Penny Stocks Strategies

Powerful Strategies to Dominate Stocks

Table Of Contents

Introduction 3

Chapter 1: How to Invest in Penny Stocks 7

Chapter 2: Tips for Investing 15

Chapter 3: Common Mistakes and How to Avoid Them 21

Chapter 4: Short Term Investing 30

Chapter 5: Long Term Investing 35

Conclusion 44

Introduction

I want to thank you and congratulate you for buying the book, "Penny Stocks Strategies".

Mistaken Assumptions about Trading Stocks:

Many people believe that being successful with trading means you have to be a exceptionally intelligent or talented. They believe that only a genius can get rich off of trading penny stocks. The good news is that's not true. This book contains proven steps and strategies on how to master penny stocks, and you don't need to be highly skilled at math or even of above average intelligence to do it.

Who is this Guide Meant for?

However, this book is not meant for everyone. It's only meant for people who have a willingness to try hard and take their trading seriously. While some believe that trading is a shortcut to riches with hardly any work, that simply isn't true, and you don't get anywhere exceptional without effort. The good news is that it doesn't matter if you're a senior citizen or a student in high school. Whether you are someone who can only read about penny stocks for an hour a day or someone who has the time to study the subject for hours a day, a complete newbie to the subject or someone who already has the basics down, this guide can help you.

What does it Take to Succeed with Penny Stocks?

As long as you have a willingness to try hard and put in the time and effort, you can be successful with the information in this book. So how much should you study penny stocks if you wish to master them? As often as possible. If you are serious about becoming a successful trader of penny stocks, every bit of knowledge and information you can find on the subject will get you further along in your goal of acquiring wealth and therefore freedom.

How to Approach this Book and the Knowledge within it:

If you don't have unlimited time, simply take the lessons, chapter by chapter, whenever you can. But as soon as possible, return to the guide, finish it all the way through, and start practicing what you have learned. If this is a subject you are interested in, there's no reason to wait around to get started. Start your journey by reading this guide.

Some of What you will Find in this Guide about Penny Stocks:

When you are reading this guide, you might see a few different perspectives described. This is because investment strategies are as varied as individuals themselves, and there is no "one size fits all" technique for trading. You must, instead, create your very own plan that fits with your personality, lifestyle, and capital, perfectly. The information in this book is not meant to tell you exactly what to do word for word, but inspire you and give you the tools to create your own plans that work for your life. The key is to try out many different methods until you find the one that works for you.

Thanks again for buying this book, I hope you enjoy it!

♥ **Copyright 2016 by Jordon Sykes- All rights reserved.**

This document is geared towards providing exact and reliable information in regards to the topic and issue covered. The publication is sold with the idea that the publisher is not required to render accounting, officially permitted, or otherwise, qualified services. If advice is necessary, legal or professional, a practiced individual in the profession should be ordered.

- From a Declaration of Principles which was accepted and approved equally by a Committee of the American Bar Association and a Committee of Publishers and Associations.

In no way is it legal to reproduce, duplicate, or transmit any part of this document in either electronic means or in printed format. Recording of this publication is strictly prohibited and any storage of this document is not allowed unless with written permission from the publisher. All rights reserved.

The information provided herein is stated to be truthful and consistent, in that any liability, in terms of inattention or otherwise, by any usage or abuse of any policies, processes, or directions contained within is the solitary and utter responsibility of the recipient reader. Under no circumstances will any legal responsibility or blame be held against the publisher for any reparation, damages, or monetary loss due to the information herein, either directly or indirectly.

Respective authors own all copyrights not held by the publisher.

The information herein is offered for informational purposes solely, and is universal as so. The presentation of the information is without contract or any type of guarantee assurance.

The trademarks that are used are without any consent, and the publication of the trademark is without permission or backing by the trademark owner. All trademarks and brands within this book are for clarifying purposes only and are the owned by the owners themselves, not affiliated with this document.

Chapter 1: How to Invest in Penny Stocks

The appeal of trading penny stocks is not difficult to understand. They are pretty cheap compared to other stocks and hold the allure of large profits in the future. However, if you aren't careful, penny stocks are also a quick way to lose your valuable and hard-earned capital.

Making it your Business to be a Penny Stock Expert, Before Getting Involved:

Of course, it's perfectly possible to profit and win big when you have an understanding of how the game goes, but when you aren't aware of it, the odds are stacked heavily against you. This is especially true when you consider that scammers and manipulators are often the ones running the show of penny stocks.

For people who are interested in investment but cannot afford shares in companies like Microsoft or Google, the possibility of profiting from these types of trades are too tempting to pass up. It is this reason, and more, that the business of trading penny stocks does so well and continues, despite the risks involved. Even with giving a relatively small amount of capital, you can earn a decent profit from the return, as long as the trade goes in your favor.

Promoters of penny stocks always attach disclaimers to their Facebook pages, e-mails, or Twitter accounts, taking advantage of the words they choose to deceive and embellish facts. Promoters of penny stocks also have a tendency to stay ahead of regulations for security. Even considering these facts that make trading penny stocks risky, certain people can't resist the allure of them. So, if you are well aware of the dangers of the lies of penny stock promoters, penny stock newsletters that lie to you, and other risky factors of the game, and still wish to proceed, there are some things you need to remember.

To become Successful with Penny Stocks, Keep in Mind the Following:

1. Don't Pay Attention to Success Stories about Penny Stocks: Experts on penny stocks, people who know all about trading both short and long, tell you that you should never believe the incredible success stories that are fed to people through social media platforms and spam e-mails, however tempting they are.

No matter what, you have to ignore these stories. Get the idea of winning the lottery out of your mind. Looking at penny stocks like golden tickets to riches is the wrong way to approach this subject. Unfortunately, most people do exactly that, and it's what leads them to lose over and over again.

This is part of the reason why penny stocks have a sketchier reputation than others. Instead of viewing these stocks as your tickets to riches, think of them as shady characters that have to earn your trust. Pay attention to the penny stocks that are profitable with solid growth of earnings.

2. Read disclaimers thoroughly and don't pay attention to tips penny stocks are sold a lot more often than they are bought, and it's usually through tips from newsletters and e-mails. Newsletters talking about penny stocks are hardly going to give free tips out for no apparent reason. In fact, if you take the time to actually read the bottom portion of these letters, including disclaimers, you will see that they are being paid to promote certain stocks.

This is because their investors are in need of exposure for their companies. This is not inherently bad, and there is nothing necessarily wrong with needing or desiring exposure, but nearly every newsletter about penny stocks gives you fake promises about low quality companies. There is a distinct difference between stocks earning high for a year straight because of a breakout in earnings and stocks earning high for a year straight because a few newsletters chose it.

A lot of newsletters don't bother to fill you in on the truth since they are being paid to make the stock seem incredible rather than worthless. Falling into the trap of mistaking one for the other can be assuaged quite simply. When you read the bottom portions of these newsletters or e-mails, including the disclaimers, you will often see that there is, somewhere, a conflict of interest happening.

3.Try to Sell Fast: One huge upside of penny stocks is that you can make up to 30 percent profit in just a couple of days. If this happens to you and you earn that type of return, the best guidance you can take is to sell fast. This is where a lot of traders go wrong by getting greedy, hoping and aiming for a huge return, instead of taking what they have already made. Remember that your penny stock choice could just be getting hyped up by promoters, grab your profit, and get out while you can.

4.Don't Listen to the Management of a Company: In the world of penny stock trading, you should never believe what companies tell you right off the bat. You cannot make the mistake of trusting people easily, since companies are just trying to pump their stocks up to raise funds so their company can stay afloat and advance.

Since no accurate data or reliable model for business exists here, a vast number of penny stocks are actually scams or schemes created with the intention of enriching people on the inside of the operation. There have even been instances of big rings of individuals running separate promotions with different companies and press releases.

5. Try not to Sell Short: There are times when shorting

penny stocks that have been pumped up might seem very appealing, but one method that may bring you success is avoiding this temptation. Penny stocks are, by nature, very volatile. This means that if you end up on the worse side of things, it's possible to lose more than half of what you have.

Another issue is it's hard to discover penny stock shares that can be shorted, particularly the ones that make large moves with newsletter tipping and hyped up information. Let the pros do the shorting with penny stocks.

6. Focus your Attention only on High Volume Penny Stocks: You would be wise, especially when you are first starting out with penny stocks, to stick with the ones that trade a minimum of 100k shares each and every day. Trading stocks that have a low volume can make it hard to get out of the position you are in, which is not a desirable situation.

You need to know about the amount of shares being traded along with the volume of dollars involved. You should also look to trade stocks that are worth over 50 cents per share. Any stocks that trade less than that and are worth less than half a dollar, and don't have enough liquidity to be of any value to you.

7. Make sure to Utilize Mental Stops: Due to the spreads on the bid asks of some penny stocks are very high, even up to 10 percent at times, using stop losses in a hard sense can lead to you losing a lot of capital. It does take more effort and focus, but you need to utilize mental stops when you can. By focusing on the risk vs. reward more than stops, you will be in a better position with your penny stocks. Aim for a safe bet and always know what that is before going in.

8. Purchase only the Best of a Group: Choosing to only purchase penny stocks with earnings breakouts under their belt is a wise decision. This means that you buy them when they already have made great earnings or are getting up to a year straight of high volume that has reached a number of shares that is a quarter of a million.

These are not as hard to find as it sounds, as long as you know how to look for them. The hard part can be discovering stocks that have made yearlong highs not from schemes for pumping and dumping, but they do exist.

9. Do not trade your big positions: Something you should always be careful with is the sizing of your positions, otherwise you will have to learn the difficult way that trading big isn't always best. Give yourself a rule to not trade over 10 percent of the daily volume of any given stock. You can also make sure you are limiting the size of your share to give you an easier exit if you need it. Being able to get out of stocks is just as important as getting into the right ones at the right time.

10. Try not to Get Emotionally Attached to a Stock: All penny stock companies out there would have you believe that their story is about to change the way the world works, for the better. When you decide to enter into the world of penny stocks, it pays to be cynical about it. Also make sure you do plenty of research and be diverse about your investments. This applies even when a member of your family or close friend is trying to sell a stock to you.

A lot of people get caught up in with trading their strong emotions, which can hold them back and limit them. The best way to be successful is find out early how to get this under control so you can excel at the game. Also keep in mind that penny stocks have a sketchy reputation and that this has its valid reasons, so always be aware.

Finding Penny Stocks that will Pay you Dividends:

There are not a huge number of these, but some penny stocks do pay you dividends, and discovering them is worth the search. However, this should be seen as a way to supplement your investment returns, rather than a main income source or something bigger.

Using newsletters or websites for finding them:

Websites and newsletters about penny stocks are one of a few different resources that people use to find dividend-paying penny stocks. A simple place to begin is looking through these websites or sources or even subscribing to a newsletter of a credible source that lists penny stocks that pay dividends.

Using Stock Screeners Online to Find Dividend- paying Penny Stocks:

Another way to find dividend-paying penny stocks is by using stock screeners online, many of which are free and easy to use. These can be found on Google Finance, or places like Fool.com or Zacks.com. Utilizing a screener like this is a great way to discover long lists of penny stocks that may pay dividends. As soon as you, as the investor, make a list of your own, you can do the research necessary to figure out whether the individual stock will suit your personal strategies for investing. This process is quite easy:

Make sure to Screen Everything Out that is not Stocks:

Make sure that your screening process isn't including in it ETFs or mutual funds.

Screen Stocks out that Sell for over $5 per Share:
While individual strategies are the best method for this and investors can decide on the appropriate dollar amount for their personal plan, this is a good guideline to work with when starting out.

You will see that the next available screen has refined your search results to what you need to see; this means stocks that have payout ratios for dividends that are over 0 percent. As soon as this refinement has been applied to the search, you will have at your fingertips a list of stocks that offer dividends. Usually, this type of search will reveal up to 100 different stocks for you to look over and consider. These results can be refined even further by adding filters like volume of trading minimums. This is useful because one common issue with trading penny stocks is trouble with finding liquidity.

Great Advice and Information about Penny Stock Trading:

Although penny stocks are usually defined by having a selling price of under $1 for each share, inflation affects this definition every so often, shaking up what the meaning of a penny stock really is. This means that penny stocks usually refer to stocks that sell under $5 for each share. What this means is that some stocks, even the ones traded on major exchanges like NASDAQ and NYSE can still be called penny stocks. However, most of what traders call penny stocks are traded using Pink Sheets or the OTCBB.

Some Information on Pink Sheets Penny Stocks:

Stocks being traded through the former, which is basically just a service for quotations, do not have to register with the SEC, or the Securities Exchange Commission, which means that they are basically not regulated. This means that they are the riskiest of all of the penny stocks that an investor can get involved with.

Some Information on OTCBB Penny Stocks:

The stocks being traded on the OTCBB are typically a lot easier to find good information about and conduct research on. However, even these penny stocks are not as regulated as major exchange featured stocks, like the stocks on NYSE. A lot of the research and information found on these could be false hype that can't be logically trusted.

Because of the high risks that come along with the world of penny stock trading, discovering the stocks that do pay dividends will do a lot to help investors maximize and preserve their investment funding. A lot of penny stocks don't fail completely; they just don't do much of anything, in general. The price of a penny stock could even stay unchanged, essentially, for up to a year or even longer. When this situation occurs, the yearly dividend of even very low priced shares can help improve the loss and profit position of an investor.

Chapter 2: Tips for Investing

The rules that you should trade using are rules that will turn the game of penny stocks, which is commonly known as risky and unpredictable, into something that can be more consistent and even predictable. These tips can turn the world of penny stock trading into a venture that offers you profit every week, as plenty of penny stock traders have discovered for themselves after using this knowledge.

There is a lot of misinformation online, which everyone knows, so having a willingness to find truly beneficial information is great, and you should be proud. If you can follow along with the tips in this chapter, you will be saving yourself a lot of headache, time, and hassle. You will also avoid losing money, which everyone wants to do.

Penny Stock Trading Tips to Abide by:

- Get rid of your idealistic visions of perfection: People who promote penny stocks don't hesitate to tell you huge stories about businesses that are just about to get huge and revolutionize the entire world with their services. The problem here is that they are usually lying. If the companies involved in these penny stocks were real companies, they probably wouldn't be involved in penny stocks in the first place. They would be on AMEX or NYSE getting traded, where the other companies that meet filing standards go. They would be selling at higher prices instead of being priced like lottery tickets.

    The truth is that most of the companies that are penny stocks are destined to fail, and the chances that you will be able to spot the tiny percentage that end up growing with time are not in your favor. This means that you need to stop buying into idealistic stories, believing what you hear. You must realize the truth about trading penny stocks in order to have any success with them.

- Shift the expectations of your profit numbers: Another factor to look out for is the hype that promoters of penny stocks will give you about how fast your capital can expand and grow. Sure, penny stocks going from a dollar to 10 dollars is possible, and it is also possible that your money will double or triple in one move. But how much should you actually be aiming for? Think more .75 cents.

While you can be happy with making more than this, committing to keeping your trades modestly small, and getting yourself into and out of them when the numbers are in good order, is the better option. This will help protect you from the possibility of disaster and huge losses that plague so many other traders. If you are always in the mindset of going after huge wins, you will find yourself forcing trades that might not even exist. This is the type of mindset that will force you out of the race before you've had a chance to begin.

- Always respect the Reality of risk: One of the necessary components of managing to keep your profits (and what you lose) small is having respect for the risk involved in trading penny stocks. Oftentimes, companies that are penny stocks are not worth basic paper. Penny stocks are traded thinly since they are known for being very volatile. It is better to take your profits and losses too fast than too slow.

Stocks that you believe are heading up can go down in less than a couple of minutes, while stocks that you believe will sell short for sure can switch course faster than you can blink. A huge factor in how risky penny stocks can be is because of the fact that a lot of the companies could not meet the requirements for filing SEC; and that the individuals trading them are not big time Wall Street people, meaning they can more easily manipulate the stocks if they desire to do so. This is why penny stocks get traded on OTCBB and Pink Sheets. If they could, they would be on the big exchanges instead.

What it comes down to is that you have no way to know for sure what you are handling when it's about penny stock trading. It's possible that the press releases you see about the new technology of a company could be legitimate, but it's also possible that these are lies invented by a promoter trying to hype up the stock. This risk is just part of the game, and not something to fight. You can, however, respect the risk.

Be sure to never commit too large of a portion of your investing portfolio to one single trade, and also ensure that whichever position you're taking isn't big enough to have an effect on the price action of the stock. Always be on the lookout for quality liquidity in penny stocks, meaning a minimum of 100k shares traded per day to give you a good amount of volume for trading. This is the only way you will be able to go into and out of trades as you need.

- Using a journal for trading: When you start trading as a beginner, a huge favor you can do for yourself is to make a journal for trading that mentions every move you make, the size of the positions you take, the profits or losses of your trades, and more. This journal will serve as a valuable teacher about both your own habits and attitudes and trading, in general. This is a must if you wish to become a trader who profits consistently.

The traders who enjoy the most consistent success have methodical strategies. They never enter trades or make a play on momentary whims. Instead, they consider their actions of the past careful and use that experience to enhance their future actions. Recorded info about your trades from the past will be extremely useful to you as you seek to move up in trading penny stocks.

If you want to maximize the usefulness of this tool, you should track your actions from the very beginning. Get into the habit now, while you are still new to penny stock trading. You can go the old-fashioned route and use a paper and pencil, or utilize an app to record your information. Whichever way you decide to do it, make a commitment to keep and update your diary each time you take action with a stock.

- Don't get so wrapped up in the game that you neglect your own health: People can get so obsessed with this world that they end up completely forgetting about other areas of life, like physical health. Some traders even put on a lot of weight or take up bad diet habits in the name of trading day and night. Don't make this mistake!

  Sure, making money is great. Sure, learning about and practicing trading penny stocks can be so much fun that you get wrapped up and forget other aspects of life, but none of this matters if you are not healthy. Don't get so wrapped up in the world of stocks that you forget to get outside and eat healthy meals regularly. You will be mentally sharp, and consequently a better trader, if you prioritize your health; but you will also live longer to do more trades this way. Get rid of your bad habits right now as you are beginning your penny stock trading career so that you can rely on your health for the entirety of your career.

- Don't be afraid to invest in knowledge: Once you start learning the ropes of trading, you may be tempted to fall into a rut of believing you know all there is to know, or that you've learned most of the tricks of the trade. But, no matter how much you learn, there is always more knowledge to gain, and there is always someone above your level, no matter how good you get.

For these reasons, and others, you should make a trading education a big priority. Seek out individuals who have done exactly what you wish to do in your trading career and start learning from them as soon as possible. This way, you have a better chance of becoming the best-informed and strongest trader version of yourself.

- Figure out how to spot quality sources for learning: It's a safe estimate to say that only a tenth of the traders that exist out there are profitable consistently in their pursuits. Don't pay attention to what traders who refuse to be transparent claim in message boards or chat rooms.

  The fact is, almost all traders are going to say that they make money consistently, particularly when they are trying to get you to buy something from them. This makes it all the more important to figure out how to select your teachers in a careful fashion. So, how do you find the legitimate teachers among the scammers? The key is looking for transparency.

- Don't be afraid to ask for proof of amazing claims: If you have found a trading teacher that can't stop bragging about their giant profits or all the ways they are going to show you how to win millions, don't hesitate to ask to see proof of this. This can be tax statements or records of the trades they have won big on. You should know ahead of time that in most cases, you will either get ignored or receive an excuse about why they cannot show you this information. Do you recall the journal tip I gave you earlier in this chapter? Traders who are truly successful aren't hesitant about sharing this information with other people.

  A lot of teachers of trading refuse to show you this info, and if that is the case with a trainer you've found, you should be skeptical, at the very least. In fact, this would cause many people to walk away from the person altogether. Time is more valuable than that, and your hard earned money didn't grow on a tree. Have respect for the journey, your capital, and trading information and take the time to select a real, legitimate, and honest teacher who will be transparent with you.

Chapter 3: Common Mistakes and How to Avoid Them

With the charts, formulas, jargon, and slang of Wall Street that comes along with investing, doing this on the internet can seem like an intimidating and even scary venture. For certain investors, the idea of taking on the management of their own money is enough to overwhelm. The fear of losing capital due to making mistakes is a lot to handle. Luckily, most of these mistakes can be pinned neatly down into one of the following categories, and thus avoided with the appropriate knowledge and practice.

The Most Common Mistakes with Penny Stock Investing:

- Selling and buying too often: A big plus side to investing online is the fact that it allows investors to sell and buy stocks when they decide to do so. The downside, however, is that some of them make this constant access part of their permanent portfolio, making trading stocks into more of a liability than anything else. Having access constantly can turn certain investors into obsessives who can't stop trading even when they want to.

- Cutting the winners off too soon and letting the losers run on: The nature of the human mind can be, in some cases, your worst source of sabotage when it comes to investing in penny stocks on the internet. People tend to react in certain ways when they face particular circumstances, and a lot of those reactions end up working against you with your investments. A couple of these elements of the human mind are holding out for bad choices for far too long, and trying to cash in on positive choices far too soon.

When an investor buys a certain stock that goes down soon after, it commonly happens that he holds onto it far past the time he should have let it go, in hopes that it will return due to the quality of the company. When you go down the road of purchasing individual stocks, you have to commit to cutting losses early on. Decide on a percentage that you can stand to risk and stand by that percentage. You can then utilize protective puts and stop orders for the market.

The opposite extreme is also possible, when investors make the mistake of chasing in too soon on their stocks that are winning. Perhaps your allocation for assets is telling you to place 20 percent in markets that are emerging, so you decide to purchase a mutual fund related to an emerging market. If these markets go up in the weeks that follow, but your index fund still makes up 20 percent of your investment portfolio, you should not sell this off to secure the gains you're making. You should, instead, stick with the allocation of your assets.

- Placing attention on the price per-share of a stock: One may be tempted to draw conclusions about prices of stocks. But one stock costing $3 and another costing $400 actually doesn't say much about either one of the stocks. The cheaper stock might, in fact, cost more than the higher priced stock because it isn't growing as fast, has more risk involved, or just doesn't earn a lot in relation to the price of its stock.

  A per-share price of a given stock only has meaning if you are comparing it to something else entirely. Usually, an investor will multiply a price of a stock by the number of outstanding share to figure out the market capitalization or the market value of a company. The market value of a stock will let you know if the stock is large, medium, or small, and will tell you a lot about the valuation of the stock.

Not keeping track of returns and risks: A lot of mistakes that investors make seem so simple that they are almost surprising. Prudence has a tendency to disappear altogether in the game of investing online. A lot of traders, possibly due to the fact that it takes practice and effort, fail to take their time with seeing the amount of risk they are taking to receive the reward they hope for or expect from stocks.

One of the largest dangers of investing while being unaware of risks and returns is not being aware of whether you are harming your portfolio more than you are helping it. You could be using a lot of your own effort and time purchasing stocks individually, assuming that all that effort is worth it, only to find out that you should have been purchasing and holding mutual funds, instead. Rather than spending hour after hour studying stock chart information, you could be better off using that time to visit family, enjoy hobbies, or work on your career.

- Trusting the wrong person's advice: It can be more difficult to not get tips on stocks than it is to get tips. All you have to do is watch television, strike up a conversation with someone next to you on the bus, talk with people in the finance section at the library or local bookstore, or talk with investors on the internet. You will find that you always run into people who have beliefs about what stocks you need to purchase now, since they are about to take off very soon.

Unless you happen to be sitting next to Warren Buffett on the bus, you should probably just nod politely and forget any advice on investing you hear about from others. Stick with the plan you decided on. Other people, while well-intentioned, simply can't know your personal details as well as you do. Only you will know what works best for you.

- Attempting to earn too much profit, too fast: When you decide to become an investor, you should realize that capital is gained over time along with companies you have chosen to invest in grow their earnings and revenue. Speaking in general, stocks return up to 1 percent, annually. You might pull off boosting that number a little bit if you are smart with allocating your assets.

    However, some investors just don't think that's enough. Instead of being satisfied with their gains, they need to go chasing after IPOs, hoard penny stocks, or chase the leaders of the market. These are typically the investors who get pulled into those schemes for getting rich quick, conferences on stocks, and other promotion scams that only benefit the ones doing the promoting.

- Letting your emotions get the best of you: The stock that ends up being your very favorite is the stock that you bought at the perfect time and never suffered any losses with. You will find that you can easily become proud of these stocks. Times of second guessing yourself and doubting your choices make up a lot of the worst choices investors make.

    These individuals can get so caught up in their love for a certain stock that they will stand by it, even as it continues to plummet past the point of no return. If you allow your fears of losing and your greed for large profits take over your decisions on investments, it is essentially guaranteed that you will sell and buy at the worst times.

- Refusing to take responsibility for your own losses: Absolutely no investor in this world enjoys losing capital on stocks, but it happens to the best of us, here and there.

The way you react to this inevitability, however, is what decides who you will be as an investor. Some of them decide to seek out others to blame for their choices, such as websites to advice givers or executives of the company they invested in.

That's the wrong approach and will only slow you down; keeping you back from the immense learning potential that comes inherently in every mistake or failure with trading.

- Not being knowledgeable about tax Information for investing: A lot of people who decide to get into investing don't know about, or ignore, the advantages of saving taxes on investing. In fact, investors can enjoy very generous breaks on taxes, if they are simply aware of them. Take the time to talk to an expert when you start getting into investing. Also, keep in mind that these regulations shift yearly.

- Failing to move on quickly from mistakes: As an investor, you can't allow mistakes from your past to freeze you into inaction. If you purchased a stock and stuck with it for too long instead of letting it go at the right time, the only way to make this worse is to linger over the mistake. Instead, learn from it and don't repeat the misstep. This is the best way to continually improve and attain the goals you hope to achieve with investing.

Due to the advent of brokerages on the internet, any person that has a bank account and an online connection can start trading in a week or less. This is wonderful because it gives people the tools to get into investing on their own instead of needing to rely on experts or mutual funds for investing. But there are a few mistakes that are made by investors who are new to the game that should be kept in mind:

- Jumping headfirst into a trade: It's easy to get the hang of investment when just considering the basic theories of buying as low as you can and selling as high as you can. However, in practice, you need to be aware of what these definitions really refer to. Keep in mind that what a seller considers high might be called low to a certain buyer in specific circumstances. This should show you the way differing conclusions can be made from the very same info.

  Due to the nature of the relative market of stocks, you need to study as much as you can before diving into it. You should, at least, be aware of the basics like dividend yields, book values, the ratio for price and earnings, and more. Figure out how each of these is determined, and what the weaknesses are and where they are.

  And as you are making it a point to learn these terms, you can begin with fake money in a simulator for stocks. It's more than likely that you will discover that the real market is far more complicated than what can be expressed by a couple of ratios, but testing these out on a demo profile will help you advance to new levels in your journey.

  Keep in mind that thinking of stocks in terms of percentages instead of dollar values is the best way to go about it.

- Basing everything on one single investment: Deciding to invest all of your money in one investment is typically not a great idea. Even the greatest companies out there can encounter unforeseen problems and watch the stocks go down drastically as a result of that. Sure, there is a lot more potential for great gains when you put all of your eggs into one basket, but you are also encountering a huge amount of risk. Particularly if you are investing for the first time, you should purchase a multitude of types of stocks. This means that you can learn lessons as you go that are valuable but not devastating.

- Using cash you cannot lose for investments: Studies have proven that the money you place in the market in large amounts instead of in smaller amounts has a better return overall, but that does not mean that it's wise to invest all you have at the same time.

  Investing is something you should get into with considerations for the future, whether you trade or you invest using buying and holding. This means that remaining involved requires capital on the side that can be used for opportunities and unforeseen emergency situations. While having extra money on the side won't earn you any profit or a return, having all of your capital invested is so risky that even the most professional of investors don't do it.

  If your situation is only having enough money for investment or just using an emergency money account, you are not in the right place financially to be investing. It simply doesn't make sense in those situations. This is the type of investing that will lead to mistakes based on biases in your behavior and added the added risk of mistake-making is the last thing you want. There is already enough room for mistakes, especially when you are just starting out, without that added element.

- Relying too much on news about stocks: Whether you are hoping to find out which company will turn out to be the next Microsoft, finding quick hot stock tips to invest in, or following a clue about earth shattering profits; using news as a source for what to invest in is a horrible idea for you if you are new to the world of investing. Keep in mind that you are in competition with professionals that have access to information instantly and know exactly how it needs to be analyzed.

The absolute best you can hope for in that situation is to be lucky and hope that it keeps happening, but that is unlikely to happen continuously. The worst you can fear is getting stuck entering too late, or even following a rumor that has no basis in reality, and over, before you decide to abandon investing in general. Instead of following these news stories or possibly false rumors, your ideal beginner investments involve companies that you have an understanding of. If you also have experience personally in dealing with the company, that's even better.

You would never continuously bet on black when going to a casino with the hopes of earning profits long term, so doing this with investing doesn't make any sense either.

In Summary:

Keep in mind that when you decide to buy stocks personally on the market, this makes you in competition with huge mutual funds.

The people involved in this are investors who make this their full-time business, and it's done with a lot more information and resources than you or the average individual has access to. As you start out with investing, although it may be tempting to do otherwise, you should always begin small and only take risks using capital you won't suffer from losing. Starting too big or using money you can't afford to lose can mean that the market is harsh to you, and you may get so burned that you want to swear off investing altogether.

Once you start getting more familiar with how this field works, the most reliable ways to get quality information, your own tactics and more, you can start investing larger amounts and working with more money. A lot of people get into investing only to lose interest quickly because they do it wrong, investing too much at once, gambling on the market, or using false information in hopes of winning. It's a wise idea to invest by yourself, to find out more about how the market works. However, make sure you are investing in areas you are familiar with and always aim for stocks that have quality that you would like to hold onto for longer time periods.

Sure, it sounds appealing to make money fast, and lots of it, but that's just not how this works.

Like any other field, earning real profits comes over time from slowly building up your earnings. If you are viewing investing with the attitude of lots of money fast for little work, you may want to either reconsider getting into this or step back and think it over or wait until you are ready.

Chapter 4: Short Term Investing

Short term investing refers to holding investments for a few days to a few years before getting rid of them, in hopes for making a profit (of course). This typically takes a more active approach with watching the market closely and often as opposed to allow your money to sit and being able to forget about it for periods of time. Here are some ways you can benefit from investing in stocks short term, and heighten your chances and amounts of returns.

Investing Short Term, the Basics:

Someone who prefers to hold onto securities for just weeks or months at once (at times longer if it turns out the shares perform better than expected) is known as a swing trader. These types of traders get into the market typically only when it is going in their preferred direction, being sure to exist when the activities stop showing these types of trends. For example, a business that has been making top earnings for more than a year could be still held onto by a swing trader, since the stock continues to earn. It simply wouldn't make sense to hold onto it if it wasn't earning, right? As it turns out, it's not quite that simple.

This can be Considered a Somewhat Controversial Investment Style:

There is, actually, a better answer to the question asked above. Investing for the short term is an endeavor that involves high risk, as many advisors in the financial field will warn you. If you look at the rolling average of 15 years on stocks that are small cap, an index fund, or mutual fund, you will see that the chances of an investor making strong profits over the course of a decade is almost 90%. However, if you decide to invest for short term instead, you could be gambling or taking a large risk.

This is because investors who invest short time need to make sure they are timing the market as exactly as they can, essentially trying to predict what is going to happen in a small amount of time. This means that they must buy stocks, as quickly as they can, at their lowest rating and then turn around and sell them when they are at their highest. This doesn't give the stocks a lot of opportunities to come to a balance with their lows and highs. However, investing in the short term does have some distinct advantages to it, as long as you know about which risks come along with it and possess a quality strategy or have a quality, knowledgeable consultant to go to for advice.

Short Term Investments, the Advantages:

If, when you are starting out with penny stocks, you have less of a time horizon to work with, it's possible to benefit from intermediate pricing trends of the market, say, a few months to nine months, and get rid of risks, at least partially. Getting rid of these risks includes lessening the chance of volatility for your portfolio, avoiding huge swings in the market that are happening over longer time periods when the market starts showing downward trends.

What Situations is Short Term Investing most Beneficial in?

If you have quality insight into a company or the particular industry you are working with and also think that there are upsides to short term investing, this may prevent, also, needing to have your capital tied up for longer periods of time when you may have the need to deploy or invest it somewhere else. It's highly possible, with the right information, to effectively manage risk and enjoy big returns quite fast. However, there is a lot of disagreement out there, with consideration to the pros and cons, about investing short term versus investing long term.

Everyone has Different Ideas for What is Best:

Everyone out there has different ideas about what works best and why, and any approach will have people who disagree. For example, some managers of money disagree with the approach of Howard Bandy, a man who has created systems for trading and written about the subject in a few different published works of writing. He explains investing and trading with statistic modelling and mathematics. He likes to use the method of first evaluating and taking care of risk factors, then aiming to maximize profits, but only under a specific level of tolerance for risk.

Why can Long Term Investing seem so much Better?

One of the reasons that experts can look to the success, comparatively, of investing long term, is because of a specific period of time that was uniquely positive, after the Second World War. Before the dawning of the new millennium in the year 2000, the market for equities hadn't suffered a bad decade since the 1930s.

What should you Look for in Stocks for Short Term Investing?

According to some experts, the best and most profitable trading methods trade very frequently (up to 30 trades annually). They also only hold for small periods of time (up to about four days or so) and possess a high winning and losing ratio (up to 70 percent, to be precise). As we've mentioned a few times, trading stocks that are highly liquid is recommended, along with looking for funds that are exchange-traded.

You should focus on price actions of stocks that are in the top quarter, meaning that they outperform at least 75% of other stocks within the same peer group, or companies that are about the same size. When you are looking at approaches in an industry, pay attention to what appears to be moving up drastically. When you see a whole group go up at the same time, this is an important indication of a good investment potential. You can look for options that have been struggling for long periods of time but appear to be recovering from that period of struggle. You can make purchases on weaknesses that are short term or based on pullbacks that make sense in terms of longer upward trend motions.

What Qualifies as Short Term Investments that are not Stocks?

Some people aren't big fans of investing short term, especially when they have preferences for focusing on one stock at a time. The risks of losing in this situation are always higher than when you decide to place your bets in a dispersed fashion. This is why people who are interested in short term investing should opt for ETF. What ETF is, is a grouping of securities that have been designed to replicate closely a particular index. These are able to be traded quite easily, similar to stocks, and don't have a high of transaction fees as index funds in the traditional sense.

When a client wants to invest on a basis that is shorter term, for example, needing a holding time that is at least a few years, it may be better to use tactical investing methods. A tactical investing method is defined as a strategy that is shorter term inside of overall allocation of assets. In this specific case, it would refer to the favoring of assets over longer time. One method for doing this is emphasizing differing segments of the market, like a particular portfolio that has exposure to stocks that are large cap and may have up to 4% dedicated to cyber securities and financial emphasis.

When can Rising Interest Rates be a Positive thing to Look for?

You may also be interested in financial sectors when you see interest rates starting to go up, meaning that considering ETFs could be wise in the allocation of your equity. But, depending on the details of your choices, this could be a dangerous, careless, or aggressive choice, since some ETFs are leveraged in this area, meaning that they use debt, playing up losses in addition to gains.

This means that if the sector of finances happens to plummet, double losses can occur. For these reasons, you can use tactics that are part of bigger strategies. Say, making a commitment to stay with a financial industry that is leveraged for up to half a year, considering only its performance on a short term scale, and then revisit that decision later to decide whether or not to stick with it.

Is Short Term Investing Right for your Needs?

Only you know whether short term investing is best for you, and the best way to determine this is learning as much as you can about it. Although guides like this are helpful and a great step in the right direction, they are far from the only information you need to make such an important decision. When you are just starting out with investing, you should explore all of your options thoroughly before committing to any specific path.

Chapter 5: Long Term Investing

Typical investors usually fit into one of the following categories. They are either interested in investing for gains on a short term level, or interested in investing in gains for longer term goals. It may be obvious that both of these categories have their pros and cons, and if you are trading in the United States, tax implications differ for each and are worth looking into when making your choice. But, tax considerations aside, the strategies employed with investing short term versus investing long term can provide you with highly differing earnings and overall experiences. In the last chapter, we reviewed a bit about short term investing. In this article, we will go over some more implications of investing short term and compare those with long term investment considerations.

Some More Information on Investing Short Term:

We just covered this in the last chapter, but let's review some of what investing short term means. Investing this way usually refers to holding onto a specific investment for a short period of time. Some consider this under a year, while others will consider it less than three years. Some investors will take this more extremely, though. For example, day traders try to hold onto investments for a shorter period of time than 24 hours, starting and entering positions in the mornings and trying to exit or close them before they sign off that day or before the market closes.

This is an entirely different strategy than basic investing on a short term level. Using day trading is difficult to become good at and requires plenty of study time, practice, and more to become profitable for the average person. This chapter will compare investors who use short term methods, in regards to investments that last shorter than a year, and also investors who try to trade after only holding onto shares for weeks, months, or even up to two years at a time. Investors who use long term methods, on the other side of this equation are known to hold investments for five year, ten year, or even up to thirty year periods of time.

Selling High after Buying Low:

The main goal of most investors is to make our capital grow. To put it simply, the goal is to earn money. On the surface this sounds easy, just buy low and sell high. However, it's not that simple. People who invest using shorter trading times typically try to purchase stocks when they see that the market is having a low period or if it stands for a quality value amount. Then they attempt to sell it back after some days or even months when its value has gone back up and it promises some profit. As a concept, this sounds great, and like a solid plan that we should all attempt to do. But, as is customary with the subject of investing, this isn't as simple as it sounds on the surface.

Learning how to Time the Market as Well as Possible:

The most profitable way to maximize profits with strategies involved in short term trading is timing the market as well as you can. What this means is buying stocks at their lowest amounts and then selling them back at their highest, just before they drop back down. If you try to sell sooner than you should, you will be losing out on gain potential. However, if you make the opposite mistake and wait too long to sell, it could have negative consequences as well.

Timing the market as well as possible is something that traders who invest professionally have mastered, using advanced data analysis to project what trends will appear. For example, they might use pricing charts from historical times to look for trends that could apply to their current stock. They could make a value for their stocks, the prices they believe they are worth, and hold it up against the price currently. They could also note the values historically. They use this information to construct their plans for trading and investing. Once their stock reaches what they believe is a low point, it's time to initiate a purchase, putting their selling points at the forefront or top of the chart that records expected trending movements.

So, What is the Issue with This Method?

Problems can occur when certain shares don't end up following the trends predicted or expected, which happens all too often. At times, stocks will reach their lowest low, leading the trader to initiate a purchase, and then be forced to look on as the shares plummet even lower. Then, the investor is left to decide whether they should wait longer or sell, losing out on the hoped- for profits. As mentioned previously, the opposite occurrence can happen too, where an investor makes the purchase, sells it for what he believes is the ceiling for the stock, then watches it rise even more, and loses out on his hoped-for potential gains in profit.

Another Possible Issue with This Method:

Another problem that can occur in trading short time is the amount of trading that must happen to have positions constantly opening and closing. Even considering charges for trading that have been discounted, this can turn out to be costly, leading many investors to have trouble breaking even. Since the entire point of investing and trading is earning a profit, this is a disappointment to be avoided whenever possible, at all costs.

What Benefits are Involved in Investing Long Term?

On the other side, traders who utilize long term techniques enjoy fewer fees for trading, since they hold positions for longer time periods. Traders who use short term methods might see investing long term as boring, or at the very least, less exciting. This is okay, especially for beginner investors. But, even professional or highly experienced investors try to use the longer term strategies.

Advice from the Most Credible Expert of Them All:

Even Warren Buffett has been quoted to say that he prefers to hold stocks "forever" as opposed to for limited periods of time. To put it another way, Buffett sees the value in investing using long term methods. He views fluctuations in the market as chances and has made a lot of money by buying stocks from strong business, while others sold from fear of losing out.

What to Look for in Stocks for Long Term Investing:

Investors who wish to use long term strategies should look for companies with proven records showing growth and stability. Although new companies, at certain times, are great choices for long term profits and growth, you involve far less risk when you select companies that have already proven themselves as quality with their track records. You could also go with stocks that have strong histories of paying dividends consistently. Particularly when you can see that the company increases them every so often. Companies that have shown they are committed to paying dividends usually continue to do as they have always done.

A lot of investors will enjoy benefits from stability that investing long term gives. People who are new to the game should look first to long term methods instead of obsessively charting every shift in the market. This doesn't mean you should always purchase stocks and hold onto them

"forever" or even for decades. If you notice significant changes in the company or the entire market, of course you should use your head and make the necessary adjustments. But trades should always be conducted using your overall market principles and strategy, not always changing according to the current movements of the market.

More to Keep in Mind about Investing Long Term:

Remember your real goals here and also what "long term" truly means. Some individuals can create careers for themselves and considerable wealth from conducting trades that only last a couple of minutes. For short term trading, making solid plans based on considerable research is the best way to make and follow through with correct plans for investing. Attempting to use guesswork for predicting where the market will head is the best way to head for disaster. In fact, that's more suitable for gambling in Vegas than trading stocks. If you do consider investing short term, use caution and use only a tiny amount of your main capital. For most of you who are interested in trading, thinking of long term in your approaches is the best way to do things.

Remember that the stock market is full of exceptions to every rule, but some principles are more steady than others and hard to argue with. There are certain trends that you will notice pop up time and time again when you embark upon your penny stock trading pursuits that more experienced traders already know about. Luckily, there are some basic guiding words of wisdom you can use to utilize the long term methods most effectively.

Principles to Keep in Mind for Long Term Trading:

- Get rid of losers and allow winners to ride free: Over and over, traders take their earnings by selling off the investments they have appreciated, and then turn around to hold onto declining stocks, hoping that the latter will recover. If investors aren't aware of when to let a lower go, it could have devastating consequences. For example, they might watch the stock plummet until it is worth next to nothing. Obviously, the concept of holding onto valuable investments and getting rid of the bad ones makes perfect sense on the surface, but it turns out it's a lot harder in the moment. This information could help.

- Allowing winners to ride: Many investors enjoy huge success due to having a small stock number in their portfolio, but with big returns. If your personal principle is selling as soon as stocks have risen in value by a specific number, you might never be able to let a winner ride all the way through. Absolutely no one that sticks strictly to their numbers has had a chance to reach incredible heights.

  Try not to underestimate stocks that are doing great by limiting yourself to a pre-decided rule. Especially when you are new to this and haven't yet developed a full understanding of potential, the rules you set for yourself could be arbitrary or, at worst, holding you back from great profits.

- Getting rid of losers: You can never count on stocks bouncing back once they have started to decline. It's true that you should never underestimate quality stock choices, but it's also true that you need to be realistic about badly performing investments. It can be very difficult to acknowledge losing stocks since you also have to admit you made a mistake of judgment.

  However, you need to be as honest as you can when you notice that your stocks are not performing as you hoped it would. Never hold back from swallowing your pride, being humble, and being smart enough to move on before acquiring even more losses. In both of these scenarios, you must judge businesses using your research. In both scenarios, you must decide if prices align with the potential of the future for the business. Keep in mind, however, that you should never allow your fears to maximize your losses or limit what you can earn in profits.

- Don't let small things get to you: When you make the choice to be an investor who uses long term strategies, you don't need to panic when short term movements happen to your investments. When you pay attention to your investment activity, remember to keep the big picture in mind at all times. Have confidence in your choices and their quality instead of nervous in regards to short term volatility. And don't focus too heavily on the small difference you may save abandoning a market order and using a limit order.

    It's true that traders who are active will utilize moment to moment or day to day changes as ways to profit, but long term investing games happen as the result of altogether different movements in the market (movements that happen over the course of years). This means that you should keep your attention on the development of your philosophy for investing through acquiring knowledge.

- Choose your strategy and stay with it: It's true that different investors have different strategies for choosing which stocks they buy and fulfilling goals for investing. There are countless methods for becoming successful in this field, and there is no specific strategy that wins out against all others. But when you discover your personal style, stay with it. Investors who keep switching between strategies will not be able to benefit from the benefits of each type.

- Keep your eyes on your investment future: The hard part of trading and investment is the tendency to want to make the best decisions about unforeseeable events in the future. You should always remember that, though using past data can be helpful in signaling future events, it is the details of those future events that are the most important.

    You should always try to make your choices based on the potential of the future of a stock, rather than strictly limiting yourself to what has happened before.

- Find a perspective that considers the long term: Big profits in the short term can appeal to investors, especially investors who are new to the game. However, thinking more in terms of long periods of time will benefit these people more than having a perspective of getting in, making money fast, and getting out quick. That doesn't mean you can't earn money by doing short term active trading, but trading and investing are different methods for gaining profit on the stock market.

  Different risks are involved in trading that investors who do the buy and hold method will not experience. In addition to this, traders who are active need to have special skills to be successful at what they do. Neither one of these styles of investing are inherently superior to the other style, they both have their advantages and disadvantages. However, trading actively can be the worse choice for a person who doesn't have enough time, capital to spend, desire, or education to undertake this skill. Again, there is no objective right answer for what is best. Different styles fit with different lives and personalities.

- Keep an open mind whenever possible: A lot of amazing companies operate under names that are of the household variety, but a lot of great investments are not of the household variety. Countless small companies are capable of turning into huge companies very soon. Actually, in history, smaller caps have enjoyed larger returns than their bigger counterparts.

  So, what does this mean and how is it relevant to you? It doesn't mean that you are supposed to go out and devote all of your experience and practice to smaller cap stocks, on principle. Instead, you should keep in mind that a lot of great companies exist beyond the well-known successful types, and that forgetting about smaller companies, you could be missing out on some huge profit potentials.

In Conclusion:

Of course, no rule is set in stone with trading, and every solid rule that you operate under should be reached based on your own experience and knowledge. Regardless of that fact, these tips should be very helpful to people who decide to go the route of long term trading. These principles we have gone over (many of which are common sense) will be of great benefit to you and give you beginner insights to the right attitude to approach your investment career with.

Conclusion

Thank you again for buying this book!

I hope this book was able to help you to get your foot in the door of the world of penny stock trading. My goal was to give you as many varied tips as possible, along with general guidelines, to give you the tools to craft your very own strategy, suited personally to your life and financial situation. There is no one magical method for trading penny stocks, since different techniques will work for different people.

The next step is to test out the information given to you in this guide and find out what works for you. It's possible to earn a living and even retire early on what you make trading stocks, but it doesn't come easy. In order to be successful on this journey, you must accept that it takes time, effort, patience, and a constant willingness to learn.

Thank you and good luck!

www.ingramcontent.com/pod-product-compliance
Lightning Source LLC
Chambersburg PA
CBHW070418190526
45169CB00003B/1311